deborah ZEMKE

FASTCAR
DOODLES

THANKS
TO THE
ZEMKE CAR
GUYS.

BLUE APPLE

1. Draw four curved lines.

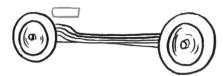

2. Draw a box near the rear wheel...

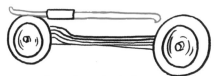

3. and attach two hooked pipes.

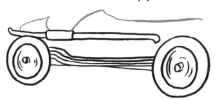

4. Make two wave curves on top...

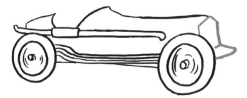

5. and a radiator of seven lines in front.

6. Draw the other two tires.

7. Pop in a driver and go!

RACE CAR

ALFA ROMEO P3 TIPO B

First from the first! With a supercharged straight-eight cylinder engine and weighing only 1,500 pounds, this red Italian speedster won its very first race in 1932.

Fast Fact *Hundreds of explosions every minute in your engine make your car go. Fuel and air are ignited in a small, enclosed cylinder, making a mini explosion. The explosion pushes a piston that turns a crankshaft that moves the power train that turns the wheels. In a straight-eight engine, eight cylinders in a straight line explode in time.*

MUSCLE CAR   *1969 BARRACUDA*

*This car has bite! With a big, bad engine in a compact body, the 'Cuda was made to tear up the road—
as long as you're going in a straight line, because it takes a lot of muscle to handle this beast on the curves.*

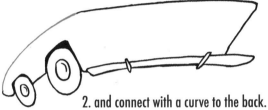

1. Attach an angle on the front...

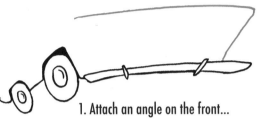

2. and connect with a curve to the back.

3. Make two mean headlights...

4. and corner them with six lines.

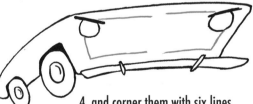

5. Draw two angles.

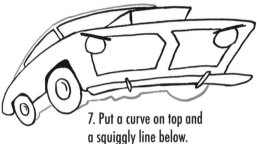

6. Put a box vent on the hood and two windows.

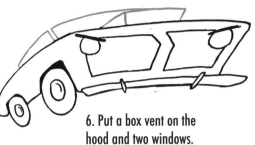

7. Put a curve on top and a squiggly line below.

8. Add teeth and a rearview mirror.

9. Add black.

Fast Fact *How do you make a fast car? You need a powerful
engine to move the wheels. But you also need a car that's light on its wheels!
The heavier the car, the harder it is to move.*

 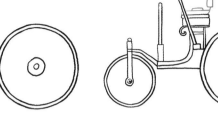

1. Add an angle to the front wheel.

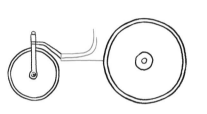

2. Attach two curves and a line.

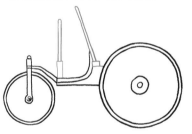

3. Make two loop handles on boxes.

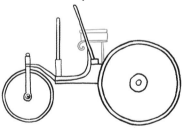

4. Draw the seat with a curl in front.

5. Make an armrest and backrest.

6. Draw a box and engine.

7. Make big spokes for the back...

8. and little spokes for the front.

The first modern automobile wasn't the fastest thing on four wheels. In fact, it only had three wheels and at top speed was slower than a horse and buggy. But with its single-cylinder, four-stroke internal combustion engine, it began the automotive revolution.

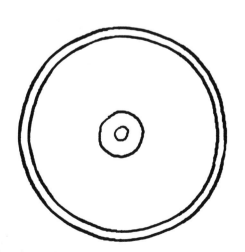

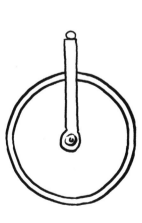

Fast Fact *Where's the wrench? In 1888, Bertha Benz took the first road trip, puttering more than 120 miles in the car her husband had manufactured. She was both driver and mechanic, fixing the car along the way with her hat pin and garter.*

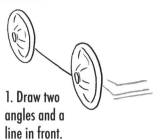

1. Draw two angles and a line in front.

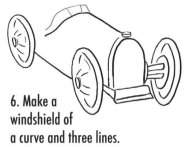

2. Connect the ends and add an arch.

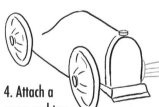

3. Draw a line, two curves, and a radiator cap.

4. Attach a curve and two bars to the side.

5. Put three curves around the bars.

6. Make a windshield of a curve and three lines.

7. Add two angles, one with a hand.

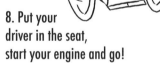

8. Put your driver in the seat, start your engine and go!

RACE CAR

BUGATTI TYPE 35

Introduced at the Grand Prix of Lyon in France in 1924, the Bugatti Type 35 won over 1,000 races in 10 years on the track! The 35B version could go from 0 to 60 mph in fewer than 6 seconds.

Not So Fast Fact

People began racing cars almost as soon as they were invented. The first organized race in 1894 from Paris to Rouen was won with an average speed of 12 mph.

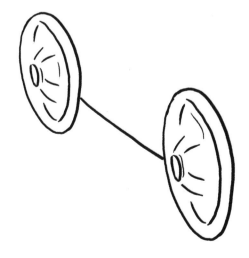

SUPER CAR ## 2011 BUGATTI VEYRON

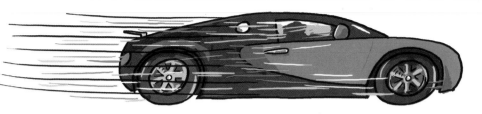

Whoosh! Don't blink or you'll miss the world's fastest street-legal production car. How fast is fastest? 267.9 mph, or more than 44.5 miles in a minute! That's one way to get to school on time.

1. Draw arcs around the wheels and connect with a line.

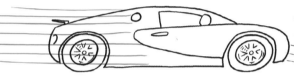

2. Make a big loopy curve from the front up and around to the back of the front wheel.

3. Attach another big curve from the top up and to the back of the back wheel.

4. Draw the curved angle window and a circular sideview mirror.

5. Add details...

6. and step on the gas!

7. I said step on the gas!

Fast Fact

The Bugatti Veyron is so hot it needs ten radiators to keep cool! The horseshoe shape of its radiator grill is the same as its great-great-grandfather, the 1924 Bugatti Type 35 race car. Of course, the newer car goes twice as fast!

1. Draw a long, straight, horizontal line. Drawing tip: when you draw a long, straight line, turn the paper so that you're drawing towards you.

2. Draw another long, curved, horizontal line that hooks back from the front.

3. Connect the front with three lines and curves.

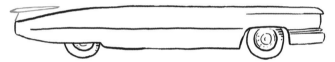

4. Start the fin with a zigzag and angle.

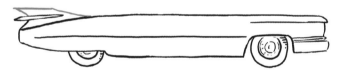

5. Finish it with three lines.

6. Put on the roof with two curves and a line.

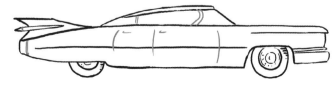

7. Add details and put it into cruise.

LUXURY CAR

1959 CADILLAC DEVILLE

Dig those tail fins! The tail fin of a fish helps it to move, but the fins on this Cadillac were just for show. As big as a boat, the Caddy could cruise up to 120 mph but was designed to glide in comfort and style.

Fast Fact *The fastest fish, the sailfish, can swim 68 mph. Its tail fin helps it move by pushing against the water.*

1. Draw two curved and one straight line.

2. Draw an angle...

3. two straight lines, and a curve.

4. Make the side window...

5. and the engine bursting out of the hood.

6. Add door, light, bumper and bed...

7. and buckle in your driver.

8. Press on the gas and brake at the same time to do a burnout...

9. and a wheelie!

Dragster Pickup /// CHEVY S10

You can turn a hard-working pickup truck into this hard-driving speed machine. But don't try to haul away brush at 200 mph!

Fast Fact *What is speed, exactly? Speed measures how fast something is going by how far it travels in a certain amount of time. With cars in the U.S., it's how many miles you would go in an hour. So if the speedometer says 100 mph, it means you would go 100 miles in an hour. If you only drove for half an hour, you would travel 50 miles.*

1966 SHELBY COBRA 427

Watch out for this SSSSSuper Snake! The 800-horsepower, twin-supercharged sports car was king of all the Cobras ever made by famed car builder Carroll Shelby. Only two were built and only one king exists today.

1. Draw a curve in the front.

2. Add a slanted 6 and a curve.

3. Make two sideways curving 6's.

4. Draw a curved hood vent.

5. Use six curves to draw the windshield, steering wheel and door.

6. Make a curvy exhaust pipe.

7. Add the back fender and tire.

8. Make your super Cobra hiss!

Fast Fact *It's not just how fast a car can go; it's also how fast a car can get going, or its acceleration. It was said that the Super Snake could get up to 60 miles per hour in just over three seconds! That's sssssscary fast!*

PERFORMANCE CAR ||| 1963 CORVETTE GRAND SPORT

Made in secret under the code name "The Lightweight," the 1963 Corvette Grand Sport was intended by its designers and engineers to put General Motors back on the racing map. But their bosses in the company found out about the secret project and stopped production after only five of these ultimate Corvettes were made.

1. Draw a flashy exhaust.

2. Put curves around the wheels.

3. Draw the fender and mid curves.

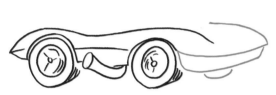

4. Make the front end with four curves.

5. Draw the roof and hood curves.

6. Make windows...

7. steering wheel, rearview mirror and hood vents.

Fast Fact *The five Corvette Grand Sports that were made were unstoppable on the racecourse, tearing up the competition for the next four years.*

 # TOP FUEL DRAGSTER

Since the race from start to finish is only 1,000 feet, Top Fuel Dragsters are designed for one thing only—to go fast fast! With a nitro-powered engine, a dragster accelerates from 0 to 100 mph in less than a second—so don't blink, because the whole race lasts less than 4 seconds!

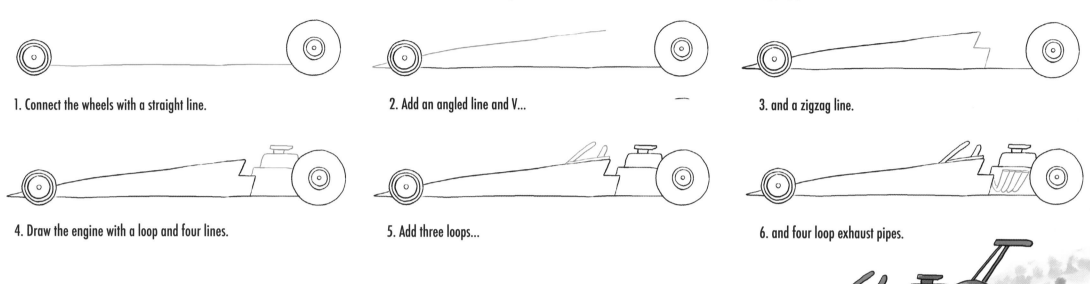

1. Connect the wheels with a straight line.

2. Add an angled line and V...

3. and a zigzag line.

4. Draw the engine with a loop and four lines.

5. Add three loops...

6. and four loop exhaust pipes.

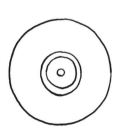

7. Draw the airfoil and gun it!

Fast Fact *These dragsters not only start fast, they have to stop fast, too! How do you stop fast when you're going 330 mph? Step on the brakes—and open the parachute!*

DUNE BUGGY

Go in the garage and make your own tube-framed or fiberglass dune buggy. Stick in an old air-cooled Volkswagen engine, some wide tires, and then hit the beach!

1. Add a curvy line on top...

2. and a curve box on top of that.

3. Draw a C bar in front...

4. and attach a wheel and a rod.

5. Make two headlights.

6. Draw two boxes...

7. surrounded by six lines.

8. Put in a driver, an engine...

9. a tall flag and go!

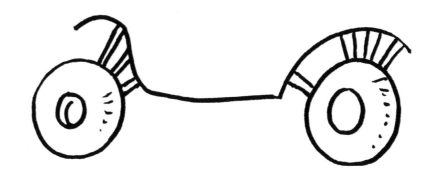

Fast Fact Stay cool! Engines create a lot of heat, and it's important to keep them cool. In most cooling systems, a heat-absorbing liquid coolant is pumped around the engine, into the radiator, and back around the engine again. In the air-cooled engines of most dune buggies, there's just cool air flowing over the engine.

RACE CAR | FERRARI 330 P4

This car was made to go—and go and go and go! Designed with a big V-12, three-valve, fuel-injected engine in a car with a wider track and shorter wheelbase, the 330 P4 was one of the speediest, steadiest, and prettiest long-distance race cars ever made.

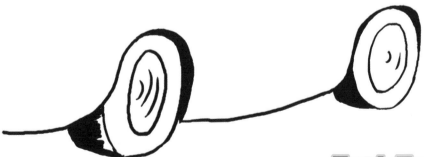

1. Draw a swoopy, backwards S.

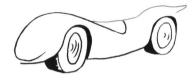

2. Make a bulging curve with a hook.

3. Add a curvy L in the front.

4. Draw a loop and part of a circle.

5. Add three curves...

6. and three more curves...

7. and two more curves.

8. Make a window.

9. Add your winning number and go for the checkered flag!

Fast Fact *Most cars have one intake valve and one exhaust valve in each cylinder. The 330 P4 had two intake valves and one exhaust valve, so it could push more fuel and air into the cylinder. More fuel and more air makes more vrooooom!*

From the front, most cars are symmetrical, which means if you draw a line down the middle, each half reflects the other. Draw the right half of this race car so that it looks like a mirror of the left half.

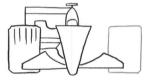
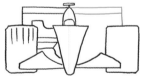
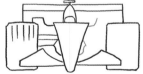
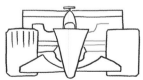
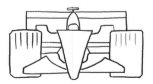

RACE CAR FORMULA 1

Imagine seeing this strange machine in your rearview mirror! Is it a car or an extraterrestrial spaceship? Formula 1 race cars are high tech, ultralight single-seaters with open wheels and such powerful engines they can literally fly off the track! The airfoil wings in the front and back are to help keep the car on the track—not in the air!

Fast Fact *Don't try this at home! Formula 1 drivers steer their cars around a track at up to 200 mph while lying down.*

HONDA DREAM

With electric motors powered by the sun, solar cars may look like futuristic fantasies, but they are in a race all their own. The Honda Dream won the 1996 World Solar Challenge, driving over 1,800 miles across Australia at an average speed of 56 mph.

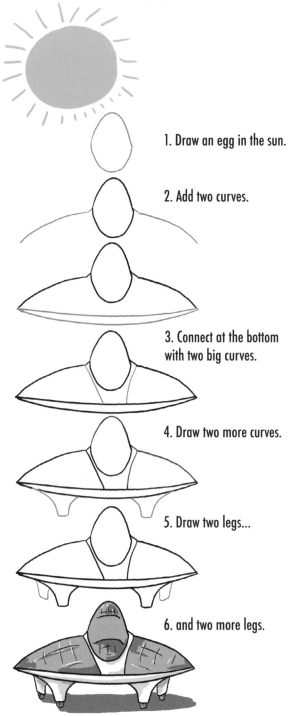

1. Draw an egg in the sun.

2. Add two curves.

3. Connect at the bottom with two big curves.

4. Draw two more curves.

5. Draw two legs...

6. and two more legs.

7. Add wheels and solar panels. Fill it up with sunshine!

INDY RACE CAR

Indy race cars are high tech speed machines that race on oval tracks, street circuits, and racetracks. The Indy 500 race is 500 miles around a 2.5 mile track. Imagine driving in a circle 200 times at 200 mph!

1. Draw a line between the two wheels and a box in back.

2. Add a curved box in front and a curve.

3. Make a wave in the middle.

4. Draw a curve and an angle.

5. Draw two curves.

6. Make the windshield and airfoil.

7. Draw two lines and a curve.

8. Put in a driver and race for the checkered flag.

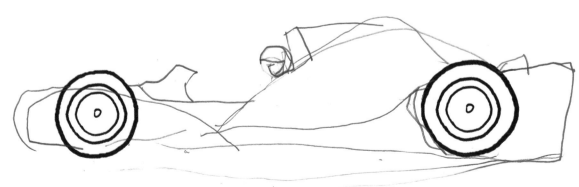

Fast Fact *A checkered flag is easy to see but hard to capture!*

1. Draw two sleek side curves.

2. Put a slanted 6 in front for the grill...

3. and another 6 for the headlight and fender.

4. Make a curved hood and soft triangle headlight.

5. Add a bumper of two loops and a third tire.

6. Draw three curves for the second headlight and fender.

7. Add a circle, curve and loop in the back...

8. and line and curve on the top.

9. Make the windshield, window, and front details.

SPORTS CAR ||| *JAGUAR XKE*

This powerful cat made a Sunday drive in the country as exciting as a first-place finish. Built like a race car, the Jaguar XKE could pounce from 0 to 60 mph in just over 7 seconds. With its smooth supension and syncromesh gearing, it roared over hills and through curves in sleek style.

Fast Fact *I like the way you shift those gears! Power moves at a high speed from the engine to the wheels through the transmission system. The gears control the speed, so a car can go slow and fast, and stop and start and go.*

SPORTS CAR ||| *1969 LOTUS ELAN*

1. Draw a line around the front wheel and back.

2. Attach a loop.

3. Draw two curves in front...

4. and a big curve from front to back.

5. Add two curves to the front.

6. Make the windshield, door and headlight.

7. Add black...

8. a driver, and hit the road!

Colin Chapman, the founder of Lotus, said, "Adding power makes you faster on the straights. Subtracting weight makes you faster everywhere." With a zippy engine and fiberglass body, the 1,420-pound Lotus Elan was big fun in a small car.

Fast Fact *The chassis is like the skeleton of a car, the frame that supports everything else. Usually it's a rectangular ladder frame with tubes from front to back on each side, and the axles running across from wheel to wheel. The Lotus Elan had a backbone chassis, one main tube running down the middle.*

LOWRIDER

Who wants to go slow? When you're cruising, low and slow is the way to go! Lowriders are designed to ride low to the ground with flashy paint, booming sound and custom comfort seats.

1. Draw a line from the back around the front.

2. Add three small circles in a line underneath.

3. Draw a line and a box in the front and the back.

4. Make a tail fin with a curve and line.

5. Add a curved box and a line.

6. Draw the side view mirror.

7. Draw a line across and down the front with a box.

8. Make a big side window...

9. and the roof. Paint your car with cool flames!

Fast Fact Lowriders can go up and down with the flip of a switch using a hydraulic suspension system.

CROSS COUNTRY RALLY CAR

This Mini goes maximum! Racing hundreds of miles over tough terrain, cross country rally cars are built to keep going, in races that can last two weeks, across deserts and over mountains.

1. Draw a curve above the wheels.

2. Add headlights and a grill.

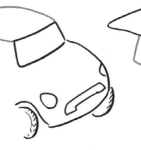

3. Make a windshield...

4. and a roof.

5. Attach a window and side view mirror.

6. Make a vent for the side...

7. and a vent for the roof.

8. Add racing stripes and clouds of dust.

Fast Fact *Which way is the checkered flag? In cross country rallies, two heads are better than one—one to drive and one to find the way!*

Brute strength! Monster trucks are twice as big as standard pickups, with 1,600-horsepower engines that are 10 times as powerful.

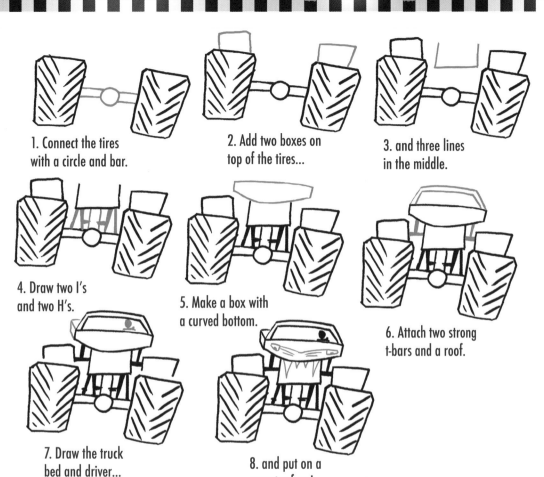

1. Connect the tires with a circle and bar.

2. Add two boxes on top of the tires...

3. and three lines in the middle.

4. Draw two I's and two H's.

5. Make a box with a curved bottom.

6. Attach two strong t-bars and a roof.

7. Draw the truck bed and driver...

8. and put on a monster face!

Fast Fact These monsters can jump! But what happens when they land? To soften the landing, monster trucks have super strong suspension systems of springs and shock absorbers.

MONSTER TRUCK 2

Monster truck tires are BIG. For racing, tires must be 66 inches high and 43 inches wide, which is taller than the average 10-year-old!

1. Add shocks to the two wheels.

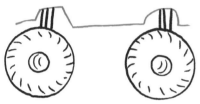

2. Draw a bending, curving horizontal line.

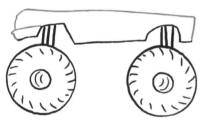

3. Add a front bumper and a long curved line.

4. Make the top and back.

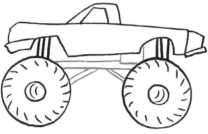

5. Draw a box and three bars underneath.

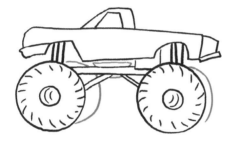

6. Add three curves behind.

7. Finish with a driver and detailing. Don't forget to give your monster plenty of support.

Fast Fact The world's largest tire, an 80-foot Uniroyal Giant, never rolled down the road. It was made as a Ferris wheel and now is a roadside landmark near Detroit, Michigan.

PERFORMANCE CAR /// FORD MUSTANG

First in a long line of Mustangs, the 1965 Ford pony car was fun, fast, and affordable. On the track and on the road, it was a sensation, creating a trend for good-looking cars that could kick up their wheels!

1. Draw a line from the front wheel to the back.

2. Add a curve and loop to the front.

3. Make two headlights and a grill.

4. Add curved fenders over the headlights.

5. Make a curved hood vent.

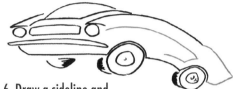

6. Draw a sideline and back.

7. Add the curved roof...

8. windshield, and window.

Fast Fact Why talk about horsepower if there are no horses under the hood? Horsepower measures the power of the engine. An engine with one horsepower can move 3,300 pounds 10 feet in one minute. A 1968 Mustang with a 427-cubic-inch V-8 engine has 390 horsepower and weighs about 3,300 pounds. So the mighty Mustang can go 3,900 feet in one minute.

FANTASY CAR /// NUCLEAR CHARGE

1. Add two curved lines to one headlight.

2. Attach a big C curve.

3. Draw a curve and a slice.

4. Make two angles and a curve.

5. Draw a curve, two short lines...

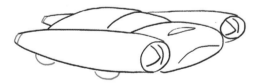

6. and six small curves.

7. Add windows and a robot driver, and blast off!

Fuel of the future? There are nuclear-powered submarines, so why not a nuclear-powered car? You would only need to fill up your nuclear-powered car every three years. That would save a lot of trips to the gas station. But what happens in a nuclear-powered car accident? And what if your car started glowing in the dark?

Fast Fact *A power plant on wheels! A car equipped with a small nuclear reactor could be used to power an electric engine or a new-fashioned steam engine.*

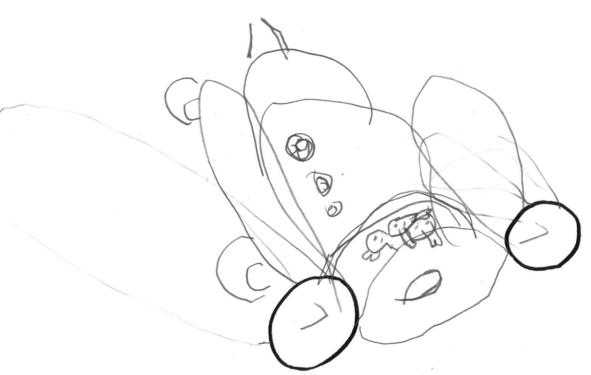

1. Draw a line over the front wheel and behind the back.

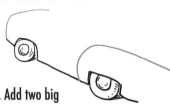

2. Add two big curves.

3. Draw a line and a curve.

4. Make windows and the trunk.

5. Add rear lights and a fender.

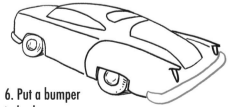

6. Put a bumper in back.

7. Add details...

8. and a tailpipe, and race to the stars!

STOCK CAR ||| *1949 OLDS ROCKET 88*

Out for a Sunday drive at Daytona Beach? The cars running in the first stock car races were just like Mom and Dad's. Well, maybe souped up, just a little. The Olds 88 rocketed to stock car success, winning 85 races in 10 years with its revolutionary V8 Rocket engine that made it a winner on the track and in the marketplace.

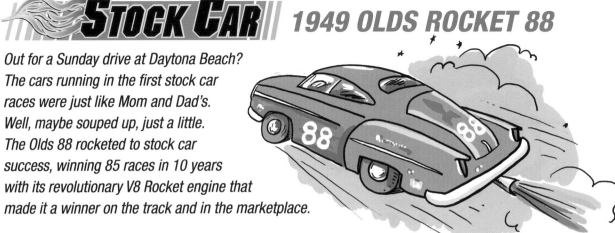

Fast Fact *Don't forget the sunscreen! The first stock car race was at Daytona Beach—right on the beach!*

SPORT MOTOR BIKE

Around a track, off the road, over hills, on dirt, pavement, open roads, closed tracks, through woods, cities, even indoors, motorbikes of all kinds race to see who's the fastest on two wheels. Some races run hundreds of miles and take days or weeks, and some are over in seconds.

1. Draw a box and a line.

2. Make two angles.

3. Draw a zigzag line...

4. and attach a curve to it.

5. Draw an I and a C.

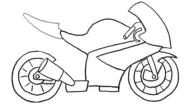

6. Attach a swoopy curve.

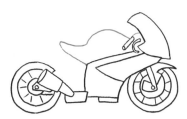

7. Make a curve and a wave.

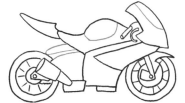

8. Draw four curves.

9. Draw three tears, a circle and curvy i.

Fast Fact It's an Ack Attack! That's the name of the world's fastest motorcycle. With two engines and a record-setting speed of 376 mph, the Ack Attack is the fastest thing on two wheels.

STOCK CAR

PLYMOUTH SUPERBIRD

With a high rear wing and downturned nose, the streamlined Plymouth Superbird could fly! The Superbird and its brother, the Dodge Daytona, looked like the future for stock car racing in 1969. The Dodge blazed a record of 201 mph. Then the rules were changed so the two cars could only race—and win— for two years.

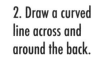
1. Connect the wheels and add a C to the front.

2. Draw a curved line across and around the back.

3. Draw three lines...

4. and two curves.

5. Make the windshield and window...

6. and attach the roof.

7. Draw three lines and put a bar in back.

Fast Fact *Speed is in the air! It's not just the engine that makes a car go fast. It's also what doesn't slow a car down. A car moving forward pushes through the air. The more smoothly it pushes, the faster it goes.*

8. Attach the wings and fly!

1. Connect the wheels and add a curve in front and back.

2. Make a muscle...

3. and two big hooks.

4. Add the bumper and grill...

5. headlights, tire, and fender.

6. Draw the roof and windows.

Looking for muscle? Put the largest possible engine into the lightest possible midsize car. No frills—no power seats, windows, steering or brakes—just raw horsepower. The 1964 Pontiac GTO laid down the tracks for high performance in a street car, amping up to 60 mph in 6.5 seconds.

Fast Fact *Hear me roar! The sound of the engine goes out through the exhaust system, along with leftover gases. The more powerful the engine, the more air and fuel are ignited, and the more leftover gases that you need to get rid of fast! The GTO's dual exhaust made a mighty roar!*

1. Draw a line around the front wheel and up to the back wheel.

2. Draw two straight horizontal lines.

3. Add a curve in the front...

4. and two curves in the back.

5. Make the tail fins.

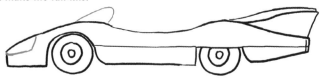

6. Draw the headlight and windshield.

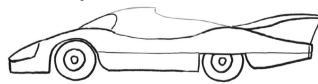

7. Attach the top...

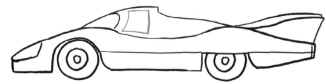

8. and make the driver's window.

RACE CAR ||| *PORSCHE 917*

How fast could you go for 24 hours without stopping? Speed and endurance of both cars and drivers have been tested at the 24-hour Le Mans race since 1923. The Porsche 917 was the first of many winners for Porsche, with a top speed of over 240 mph.

Fast Fact *Who's the fastest driver NOT on four wheels? At the start of the Le Mans race, the drivers sprint to their cars, jump in, start their engines, and take off for the 24-hour car race marathon.*

1. Draw a line up, around, down, over, up and down.

2. Make a box in front...

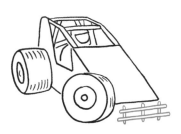

3. and a box on top of that...

4. and a box on top of that.

5. Make the rollover cage..

6. and put your driver in.

7. Draw the front tube bumper...

8. and two wheels.

9. Add your lucky number and lucky stars and kick up some dirt!

SPRINT RACE CAR

These high-powered midgets race 25-50 laps at over 140 mph on dirt or paved oval tracks. Since some tracks are only a half mile around, the drivers have to turn, turn, turn!

Fast Fact *Racetracks are made in all shapes and lengths. Some are ovals with four corners and two straightaways. Some are all twisting curves and turns. Sprint car races are on short oval tracks, either dirt or paved.*

T-Bucket Hot Rod

The Ford Model T was the first mass-produced factory car and became a farm and family favorite. Now it's a favorite for hot rodders to turn into supercharged, fuel-injected, fantasy machines.

1. Draw a swervy S exhaust pipe.

2. Add three more pipes.

3. Attach the engine...

4. with the supercharger on top.

5. Make a headlight...

6. and a radiator top.

7. Draw the cab...

8. windshield, steering wheel, and driver.

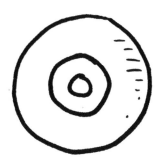

Fast Fact *The Model T was made for the rough roads of 1908. It had a top speed of 45 mph, but more importantly, it could rumble through a farmer's field, cross a stream, or climb a hill like an all-terrain vehicle.*

SUPERSONIC CAR //// THRUST SSC

The world's fastest car looks like a rocket and takes off like a rocket, too! Faster than the speed of sound, the Thrust SSC blew 763.3035 mph on October 15, 1997 to claim the World Land Speed Record. No one on four wheels has gone faster since.

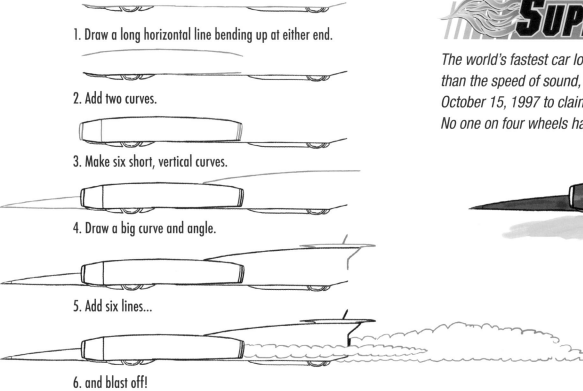

1. Draw a long horizontal line bending up at either end.

2. Add two curves.

3. Make six short, vertical curves.

4. Draw a big curve and angle.

5. Add six lines...

6. and blast off!

Fast Fact *How fast is the speed of sound? It depends on the temperature! The colder the air, the slower the speed of sound. On earth, sound waves travel 761.2 mph, while high in the frigid atmosphere, the speed of sound may be only 700 mph. So a car has to move faster than a jet to break the sound barrier.*

1. Draw three curves.

2. Add two more.

3. Draw four lines.

4. Finish the airfoil tail.

5. Make two tires and eyes.

6. Draw a driver...

7. and teeth, lots of teeth!

FANTASY CAR ||| TURBOSHARK

Want to go fast? Put on a sharkskin suit! Sharks are covered in V-shaped scales that are like teeth, with an outer enamel layer that channels the water smoothly over the shark's body. That helps the shark to move swiftly and silently through the water and makes a shark's teeth dangerous from every angle.

Fast Fact *By pushing more air and fuel into the combustion chamber, a turbo charger makes a bigger bang for the buck! And it does it by recycling the engine's exhaust gases.*

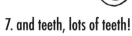

1. Connect the wheels and make a curvy curve in the back.

2. Draw a long curve over the top...

3. and attach another around to the front.

4. Make two curves in the back...

5. and an S curve on the side.

6. Draw a swoopy wave roof...

7. a wave window and wave headlight.

8. Make a driver and wave good-bye!

Is this the wave of the future? A car that floats! Imagine driving across the Pacific Ocean on your way to a surf holiday in Hawaii.

Fast Fact *The Amphicar was both car and boat, with wheels and propellers. President Lyndon Johnson had one and as a joke liked to drive visitors to his ranch down a hill and straight into a lake, shouting, "No brakes!"*

FANTASY CAR ||| ZAPTOR

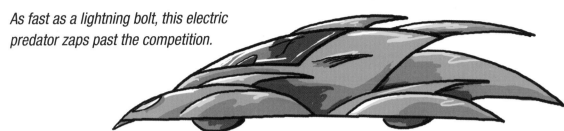

As fast as a lightning bolt, this electric predator zaps past the competition.

1. Draw two curves.

2. Add two skinny waves...

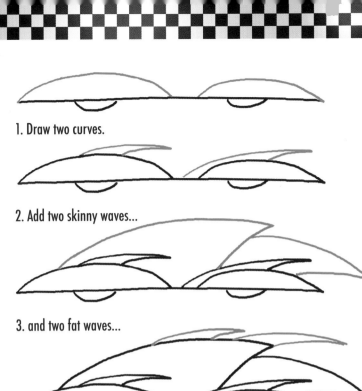

3. and two fat waves...

4. and two skinny waves.

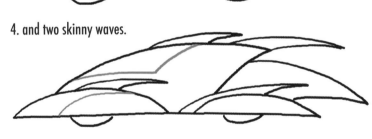

5. Draw three curves...

6. and finish the details.

Fast Fact *Where's an outlet? All-electric cars are powered by batteries that need to be recharged. But here's the charge—the electric Tesla Model S zaps from 0 to 60 in 4.2 seconds.*

Here are the keys to your new car. It goes like a rocket and handles like a dream. You can make it all your own with custom wheels and paint.

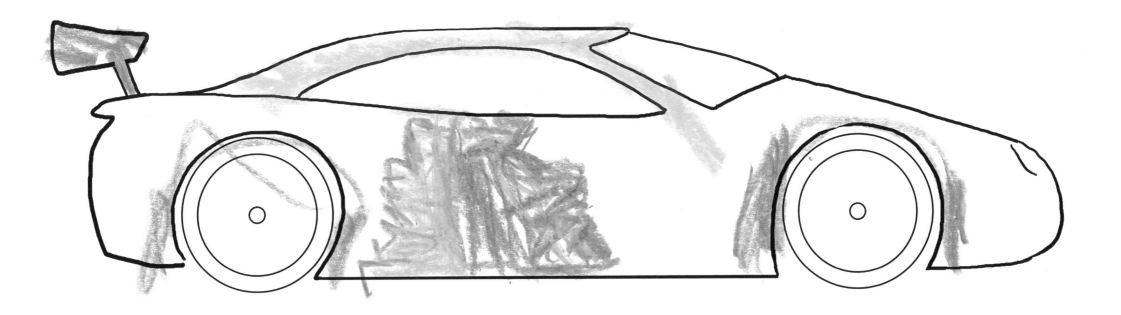

Fast Fact Going in circles? Just because all wheels are circles doesn't mean they have to look the same. Here are some ideas for custom wheel designs. Look at cars—and plants, flowers, lights, and patterns—for more ideas.

Drawing Tip It's hard to draw the same shape around a circle. To make it easier, turn the page so that you're always drawing your shape right side up.

MY FANTASY CAR

What's your fantasy ride? Starting with these wheels, draw a side view of the car of your dreams. Is it a V-12 supercharged nitro beast? Or a sweet two-seater made for the twists and turns of a hilly countryside? Or maybe it's a car that can really fly—a car and plane all in one. Name your car something fast and cool.

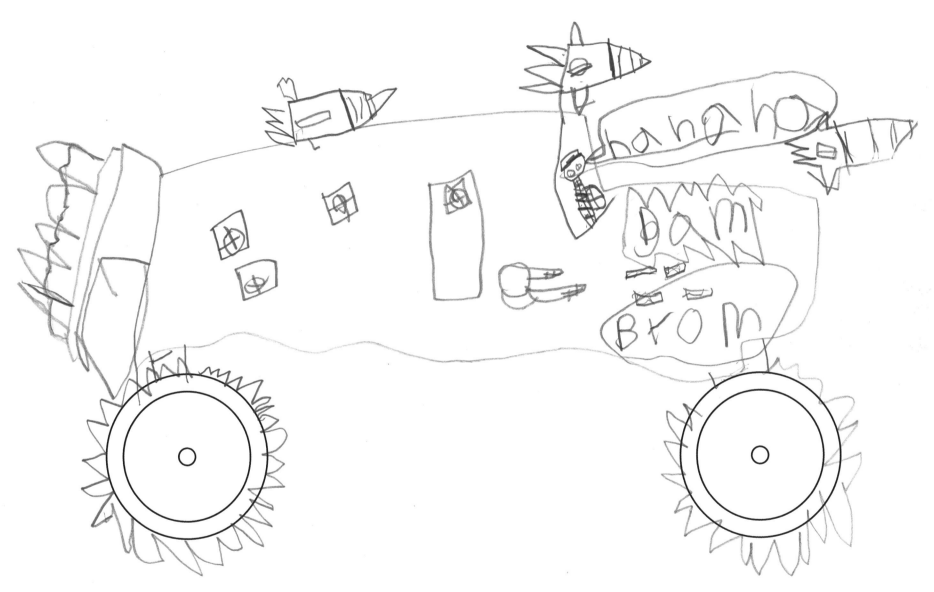